POEMS
FOR THE
HEART
& SOUL

A COLLECTION OF POETRY BY

BRENDA G. STANLEY

Dedication

In memory of my mother, Lena M. Stanley,
whose love and wisdom shaped my life.

Foreword

There are moments in life when love becomes the teacher, the healer, and the quiet voice that guides us through every season. Much of what I know about love—how to give it, how to receive it, how to honor it—was first taught to me by the woman whose legacy shaped my life: my mother. Her strength, her tenderness, her faith, and her unwavering devotion became the foundation on which I stand.

These poems rise from the stories I've lived and heard, the people I've cherished, the losses I've endured, and the grace and hope that have carried me.

These poems are not just words on a page; they are reflections of real love—romantic love, family love, friendship, community, and the sacred love that comes from God.

I write for the heart and the soul because that is where truth lives.

I write for the ones who have loved deeply, lost deeply, hoped fiercely, and prayed their way through dark nights.

I write for the ones who know that love is not always easy, but it is always worth it.

Every poem in this collection is a moment—captured, honored, and offered back to the world. Some pieces celebrate joy. Others acknowledge pain. Many speak to legacy, resilience, and the quiet courage it takes to keep loving in a world that can be unkind sometimes.

My hope is that as you turn these pages, you find something that speaks to your own journey. Something that reminds you of who you are, who you've loved, and who has loved you. Something that encourages you to keep giving, keep growing, and keep believing in the power of love in all its forms.

Thank you for holding this book in your hands.

Thank you for allowing my words to meet you where you are.

And thank you for honoring the legacy of love that continues to shape my life and my work.

Whenever you need the right message…

I got the words you need.

Brenda G. Stanley

Contents

SECTION I

Forever
Love

I Want A Forever Love

I want a forever love—
a love not dampened
by time
or the trials we face.
I want a love that forgives
and knows the meaning
of grace.
I want a love that is real
and strong,
yet gentle enough
to amend any wrongs.
I want a love that blossoms
with each season
and needs no greater reason
to celebrate
than the joy of loving
and being loved.
I want a forever love
with you.

When Somebody Loves You

When somebody loves you,
you can see it in their eyes—
in the loving glances they make
even when you are not looking.
When somebody loves you,
you can see it in their smile
and the way they light up
in your presence
or at the mention
of your name.
When somebody loves you,
you can feel it in their touch
and in the thoughtful things they do
even without being asked.
When somebody loves you,
you can hear it in their voice—
and even when they say nothing at all,
you can hear it
so loudly.

Needed & Wanted

Don't take me lightly,
as though my being here
on this earth,
at this time,
in your life,
is ordinary
or routine.
I am here
because I need you
and I want you
in my life—
and you need me,
and I believe
you want me too.
Somehow our paths crossed
so, you could give me
what I need
and I could give you
what you need.
Time and experience

have rooted us
and enriched us
beyond measure.
You have given me
more laughter,
more joy,
more love,
and more hope
than I could have ever known
alone.
And I don't take you lightly—
not for one second,
not for one day—
because your being here,
on this earth,
at this time,
in my life,
is a blessing.
You are needed
and wanted
because you are loved.

How Do You Spell Love?

L — Liberating
O — Open
V — Vulnerable
E — Everlasting
This is what
I have with you.

Untitled
(Summer Sun)

Your love is like

the summer sun

kissing my face.

It warms me

like a fireplace.

It soothes my soul

like hot water springs.

It makes my heart

weep

and sing.

It tickles my ears

like the whispering wind—

and I fall in love with you

again

and again.

Love Of My Life

You are the love

of my life

and the friend of my soul,

the honest sage

who speaks so bold,

who listens

with the heart

and gives

the best advice.

I don't know

what I would do

without you

in my life.

Unmovable Love

Love is not love
that comes and goes
when nights are long
and cold.
Love endures
the hardest days.
Through the good
and the bad,
love stays.
I will always be here
to see you through—
because I truly
love you.
Unmovable.
You and me.
Forever.

I Chose You
(Mountain Climbers)

I chose you
because you chose me—
to travel together
as companions
through life.
Although we have
our own ambitions,
goals,
and desires,
we choose to share
our lives,
dreams,
and days.
And I hope
it is forever,
because my journey
is more fun,
richer,
and more promising
because of you.

Sunrises, Sunsets, & Storms

I'm looking forward
to sharing
my sunrises
and sunsets
with you
forever.
And I hope
we can dance
in the rain
and weather storms
together.
For I know
my journey
will be brighter
and my load
lighter
walking through life
with you.

When I Think Of You

When I think of you,

I can't stop

smiling.

And when I hear

your voice,

I melt.

And after

all these years,

I still feel

the same way—

so in love

with you.

I Love Spending My Days With You

I love spending
my days
with you—
whether we are
sitting in the park,
talking on the phone,
or watching TV—
I love having you
next to me.
Life brought us
together,
and I hope
it is forever,
for you mean
the world
to me.

SECTION II

Black Love, Legacy & Community

When A Black Man Loves

The love of a Black man
is like the vertebrae
that hold the body straight.
It supports the bones
that give frame
and carries a name
spoken by kings.
His blood flows
like a river
through his children's veins
from generation
to generation,
raising a nation
of kings and queens.
Wisdom reigns
when a Black man loves—
his mind deep,
contemplative,
vigilant—
nurturing his children,

building his community,
and shielding his people
from harm.
When a Black man loves,
you can hear it
in his heart
as it beats
smooth rhythms
of strength
and life.
When a Black man loves,
Black women rise
and rest
in his embrace,
basking in a richness
greater than diamonds,
and their souls are at peace
as they smile
at the world,
inhaling
and exhaling
the sweet aroma
of life without fear
because of his love.
When a Black Man Loves.

We Only Have Time
To Live & Love

We only have time to live and love.

We only have time to hope,

even when we have nothing tangible to see,

for hope will lift us from the dark days

that rob us of the sunlight.

We only have time to love—

passionate love,

brotherly and sisterly love,

neighborly love—whoever we love,

let us love them now,

with all our soul,

while we can.

Don't hold back.

Love before death and time rob us

of warm bodies,

familiar laughter,

gentle touch,

and holy presence.

We only have time for family and friends,
for building bonds and bridges.
We only have time for hellos and handshakes,
because goodbyes are so hard.
And we only have time for sowing seeds
that will spread everywhere,
not digging ditches—
We only have time for hugs and healing,
for it connects our humanity
and brings peace.
We only have time to live.
So let us live—
for we only have this one life.
Let us live it as something more precious
than any diamond:
priceless, immeasurable.
Let us give from the treasures within us,
and receive the gifts others bring.
For life can shift in unexpected,
unwanted, unwarranted ways.
So let us flow on the river of life—
bathing in its waters,
drinking from its fountains,
inhaling every sweet aroma
while we can.
Let's just live.
Let's live with fierceness and faith,

with awe and expectation,
with gratitude and grace,
with purpose and praise
all our days.
Let us seize the richness of life
until we are so full, our cup runs over,
and we burst like fireworks
across the open sky.
For we only have time to live.

SECTION III

You Make My Day

Some people make you feel
like you are always home—
arms open,
smiles when they see you,
kind words
when you call them,
taking time to listen
even for a minute
on a busy day.
We all have
good and bad days,
but whenever I call you—
your voice,
your smile,
your kindness—
makes me feel
the love
and comfort
of home.
You make my day.

Friendship
&
Connection

Love Is More Than A Word

Love is more
than a word.
It is time
spent together—
listening,
talking,
living,
giving
from the soul.
Love is more
than a word.
It is growing
together,
yet it never
gets old.
Love is seen,
felt,
and heard—
because love
is a living word.

Friend Of My Heart And Soul

You are a friend

like a sister

or brother,

born from the spirit

of life

that connects us

to one another.

Inspired by love,

mercy,

and grace,

you are the friend

who knows my face.

You are the friend

who knows my heart

and my soul.

You are the friend

I will never

let go.

Missing You

It isn't just
the way you walk
and talk—
it's the way you smile
and laugh out loud
that makes me
love ya.
It isn't just
your sass,
but your class
and style
that flows
like the Nile.
You are
art in motion,
my aromatic potion
that leaves
your fragrance
everywhere.
So even when
you are not present,
your love
lingers here.

SECTION IV

A Mother's Legacy

Mother,
all my life
you have given me
the tools
to succeed.
You built me up
and turned me around
when I tried
to tear myself
down.
You were there
to cheer me on
when things
got hard.
You taught me
to believe
and trust
in God.
You taught me
to be kind

and give
from the heart.
The wisdom
you have given me
will never
depart.
And so today
I want to tell you
how much
you mean to me—
for your love
and devotion
made me
the person
I came to be.

Mother — [Muhth-Er]

Even Webster
does not hold
enough words
to define
a mother.
Roget's synonyms
are not enough
to capture
her heart
or her soul
of gold.
Her touch—
gentle hands
that shape
and mold.
No artist
can fully paint
the beauty
of her face,
nor capture

the grace
in her eyes.
Her voice—
the sweetest melody
the ear
will first hear.
Her love—
wider
than the world,
fathoms deeper
than the deepest ocean,
open
and limitless
like the sky.
Yes,
we can try,
but infinity
and divinity
are the only two words
that even come close
to the person
who will always
love you
the most.
Mother.

To Mom And Dad

To Mom and Dad—
it means so much when you say,
I know you can do it. Do your best.
Your words carry so much weight.
When you look at me,
I can see the hope
you have for me
in your eyes.
You have challenged me
to do my best
and always told me
how proud you were of me—
whether I came in first place
or second.
Your words
propelled me to take flight,
your voices like a choir
lifting me up.
Every time you said,
Keep looking up, kid,

or
You are somebody special,
I believed in myself
even more.
Your words alone
have helped me soar
to the highest heights
and believe
I could touch the moon.
Thank you, Mom and Dad,
for being my role models
and my loudest cheerleaders.
I am always a winner
because of you.

Here's My Hand, Dad

Here's my hand, Dad.
You can hold it close
and feel safe
and secure
like I did
when I was a kid
and you held
my hand.
You are the man
I always
aspired
to be.
You took good care
of our family.
You never
let us down
or left us
alone.
And now
that we are

all grown,
we want you
to know
that your love
made us
who we are.
So, hold my hand, Dad—
for I still want to feel
the strength
of your love.

A Brother Like None Other

I wish everyone
had a brother
like mine—
unique,
helpful,
amazing,
and kind—
whose shoulder
I can lean on
and in whom
I can confide.
I wish everyone
had a brother
like mine.
A brother
who is there
through thick
and thin,
a brother
who is also

a friend,
a brother,
who would carry me
without
a complaint—
and can be
playfully annoying
but, in my eyes,
still a saint.
I wish everyone
had a brother
like mine.

I Love You To The Moon And Back

Grandma,

if you counted

all the grains

of sand,

there still

wouldn't be enough

to show

how much

I love you.

You have raised me up

and given me

unconditional love—

and tough love—

to help shape

who I am

today.

There are
not enough words,
nor enough time,
to express
all that I love
about you.
So now,
in this moment
and every day,
I am thinking
of you.
Thank you
for being
so good to me
and creating
so many
wonderful memories.
Grandma,
I love you
to the moon
and back.

Sister Love

You are

my best friend,

my best adviser,

my best competitor

and motivator.

You are

everything

to me—

and I hope

you know

that I love you

more than words

could ever

say.

SECTION V

Resilience, Faith & Survival

I Am Still Me

These are the breasts
where my firstborn nestled
and suckled the milk
and honey that flowed,
nourishing her body
and soothing her soul.
These are the breasts
where the love of my life
gently caressed—
a symbol of my womanhood,
a mark of beauty,
a part of me that budded
like the petals of a rose.
These are the breasts
that made me look so elegant
in my silk blouse
and even in my old t-shirt.
I now look at them—
these breasts
that never reached

the age of sagging.
I look at my chest
where they once were,
now gone,
removed by the surgeon's knife
because of the invasive carcinoma
that hardened the softness
where my baby used to lay
her tender head.
A scar is there
where they once were.
My breasts are gone,
but I am still here—
and my daughter
can still lay her head here
when she wants to reveal
her heart.
For I am still her mother.
I am still a sister,
a daughter,
a wife,
an aunt,
a friend,
and a grandmother.
My heart still beats strong,
because though cancer
took away my breasts,

it could not take away
my love,
my self-worth,
my joy,
nor my purpose.
For I can still give,
and I am still me—
but stronger,
happier,
and whole
in a special way.
My breasts,
a symbol of my femininity,
now gone—
but I am still here,
and I am still feminine.
I am still beautiful,
still sensual,
and still lovable,
because
I am still ME.

Faith

It looks beyond
my inadequacies
to the realm
of my possibilities.
It draws on
my capabilities,
making my hopes
realities.
FAITH

Celebrating You, Celebrating Life

You made it!
You came out!
You survived!
You can shout!
You can live!
You can give!
You can move
and breathe
and have your being.
You have a new way
of seeing yourself—
whole and strong,
tried and true.
You are even
more beautiful.
You can think,
and grow,
and love.
You are more
than you ever dreamed

of becoming.
You are a star.
You are a light.
You have faced
the darkest night,
but hope and courage
carried you
when you did not see
your way through.
Through the tunnel
to the light!
You are going to be
all right.

Kiss The Living

Kiss the living,
not the dead.
Say the words
that should be said.
Say I love you in their ear
while they can know,
while they can hear.
Say I'm sorry,
let's start again.
You may not get
that chance again.
So take the chance
to give peace,
the chance to love,
the chance to reach.
While we live,
let's forgive.
Wait not until someone
has passed away.
Take the chance today

to
kiss the living,
not the dead.
Say the words
that should be said.
Say I love you
in their ear,
while they can know,
while they can hear.
Kiss the living.

Back To Us

Can we find the love we lost
somewhere beneath the hurtful words we said—
the misunderstandings tangled in miscommunication.
Where did we go wrong at that fork in the road,
you retreating one way and I another,
even though we began this journey together.
I remember when we were excited just to be together,
when seeing each other couldn't come fast enough,
when we cared so deeply, we made amends quickly.
I don't know what went wrong or how to fix it.
I don't know the perfect words to say,
but I do know I still love you.
Can we try? Can we begin again?
I just want to find my way back to your heart,
to find a way back to us,
because I don't believe our love is lost.
It just needs a tune-up, a grow-up, a fess-up, a sincere prayer,
whatever it takes—
to be rekindled into something even better,
because you are still my person.

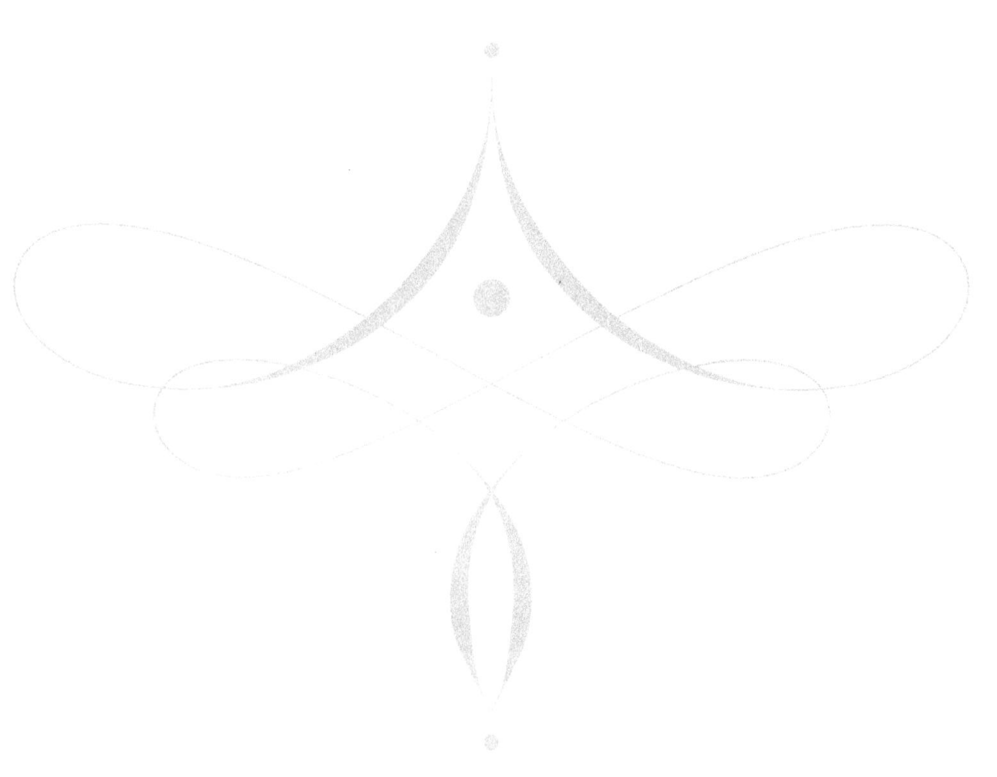

From The Author

Thank you for taking the time to read this book. It truly means so much to me that you chose to spend your time here. If something in these pages spoke to your heart, encouraged you, or helped you in any way, I would love to hear from you. Your stories, reflections, and messages are always welcome.

You can connect with me, stay updated on new projects, or reach out with questions through any of the platforms below:

✉ Anointedpoet2020@gmail.com

◎ @ispeaklifelines

𝕗 Brenda Stanley

▶ @brendastanley2844

♪ @brendastanley13

E Lifelineslegacy.etsy.com

I share encouragement, poetry, inspiration, and updates through these spaces, and I would love for you to join me there. Thank you again for reading and being part of this journey.

Brenda G. Stanley

Grace carried me, love shaped me,
and my soul keeps rising
because humanity still inspires me.

Brenda G. Stanley